TED AND TOM

FLY AWAY

Written by Shannen Yauger

Illustrated by Vanessa Toye

TED AND TOM

FLY a PLANE

THIS
WAY
UP

Ted and Tom find a big box.

"What can we make?"
asks Ted.

They get a lot of stuff.
Mom helps the boys.

"We will be back," Ted says to Mom.

"See you soon," Tom yells.

The boys fly the plane
up in the sky.

They fly past the
blue birds.

They fly past the hills and tall trees.

They see a big river.

The river goes fast.

Rocks and trees are in
the river.

"Do you see that?"
Tom asks.

"It is a small deer!"
Ted says.

"We must help!" Ted says.

They drop
down.

"Look out, Ted!" Tom says.

"We will hit that tree!"

They try one more time.

The small deer jumps.

"Yay, Ted!" says Tom.

Ted and Tom hug the
deer.

They stop on dry land by the rocks.

The deer runs away.

Ted and Tom feel good.

They hop back in the plane.

At last they
make it home.

Mom is glad to have
the boys back safe
and sound.

TED AND TOM'S
BIG KITE

Ted and Tom find a
big box.

"What can we make?" asks Tom.

They get a lot of stuff.
Dad helps the boys.

"We will be back,"
Ted says.

"See you soon,"
Tom yells.

Ted and Tom fly on the big kite.

They fly up in the sky.

"Do you see the birds?"
Tom asks.

"Let's see where they will go," Ted says.

The birds fly for a long time.

Ted and Tom fly for a
long time too.

"What was that?"
Tom asks.

"Look at that cloud!"
Ted says.

Tom frowns. That is a
dark cloud.

"Oh no!" yells Tom.
"We will get wet!"

Ted and Tom turn the big kite.

They turn away from the
dark cloud.

The birds fly away.

CRASH!

"We will tip over!"
yells Ted.

BOOM!

The boys fly fast.

"Go that way!"
says Tom.

The dark cloud is
far away.

The birds have flown away.

At last they make it home.

Dad is glad to have
the boys back safe
and sound.